SEATTL

SWIMMING
SALMON

by Kathleen Martin-James

Lerner Publications Company • Minneapolis

This book is available in two editions:
Library binding by Lerner Publications Company, a division of Lerner Publishing Group
Soft cover by First Avenue Editions, an imprint of Lerner Publishing Group
241 First Avenue North
Minneapolis, MN 55401 USA

Website address: www.lernerbooks.com

Words in *italic type* are explained in a glossary on page 30.

Library of Congress Cataloging-in-Publication Data

Martin-James, Kathleen.
     Swimming salmon / by Kathleen Martin-James.
         p.   cm. — (Pull ahead books)
     Includes index.
     Summary: Introduces the physical characteristics,
     behavior, and habitat of salmon.
       ISBN: 0–8225–0687–4 (lib. bdg. : alk. paper)
       ISBN: 0–8225–0963–6 (pbk. : alk. paper)
       1. Salmon—Juvenile literature. [1. Salmon.] I. Title.
     II. Series.
     QL638.S2 M355 2003
     597.5'6—dc21   2001005480

Manufactured in the United States of America
1 2 3 4 5 6 – JR – 08 07 06 05 04 03

This fish is a salmon.
How are salmon like other fish?

Most fish have *fins.*

Most fins are shaped like triangles.
Where are the fins on these salmon?

Fins help
fish swim
and steer in
the water.

Fish are covered with *scales.*

Scales protect the fish.

Scales can be many different colors.

All fish have narrow openings
on each side of their head.

The openings are called *gills*.

Fish use their gills
to breathe underwater.

Can you find the gills
on this salmon?

A salmon begins its life at the bottom of a *freshwater* stream.

Freshwater is water that is not salty.

These salmon are ready to *spawn*.

The female uses her tail to dig
a nest at the bottom of a stream.
The male watches over her.

The female salmon lays her eggs
in the nest.

Salmon eggs are the size of peas.
Baby salmon hatch from the eggs.

Look carefully.

Can you spot the eyes of the baby salmon in these eggs?

A salmon uses its tail
to wiggle out of the egg.

The yolk from the egg hangs from the belly of a baby salmon.

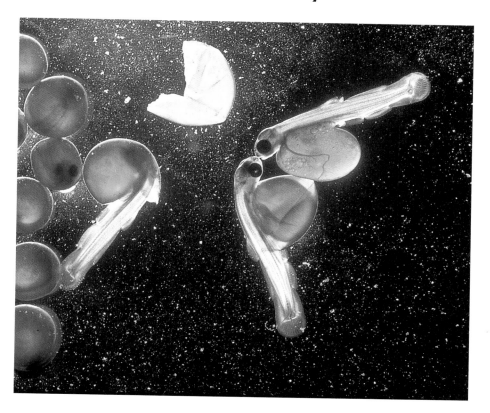

The yolk is food for the salmon.

The yolk becomes smaller and smaller as the salmon grows.

When the yolk is all gone,
a young salmon is called a *fry*.

Fry hunt for food such as insects.

Salmon grow bigger and stronger in their freshwater home.

But they will not stay there.

Most salmon swim far away
to the ocean.

The ocean is full of saltwater.

Salmon swim with the *current* to the ocean.

They swim in the same direction that the water flows.

Salmon grow bigger and stronger
in the ocean.

But they will not stay there.

Salmon leave the ocean
when they are adults.

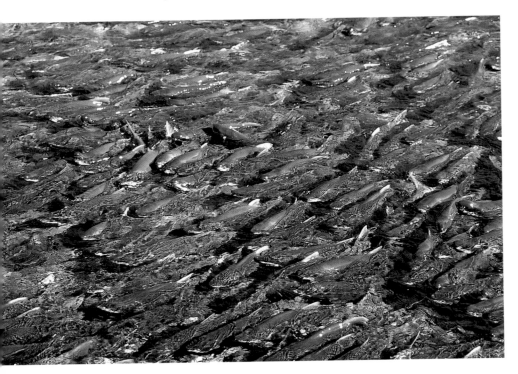

They swim back to the stream
where they hatched.

The trip back is hard.

The salmon must swim
against the current.

Salmon fight their way
up rocky streams.

They use their powerful tails
to jump up waterfalls.

Watch out!

A bear might be waiting at the top
of the waterfall.

A bear is a *predator.*
It hunts and eats other animals.

These salmon have returned safely
to their stream.

Soon the female will lay eggs,
and new salmon will hatch.

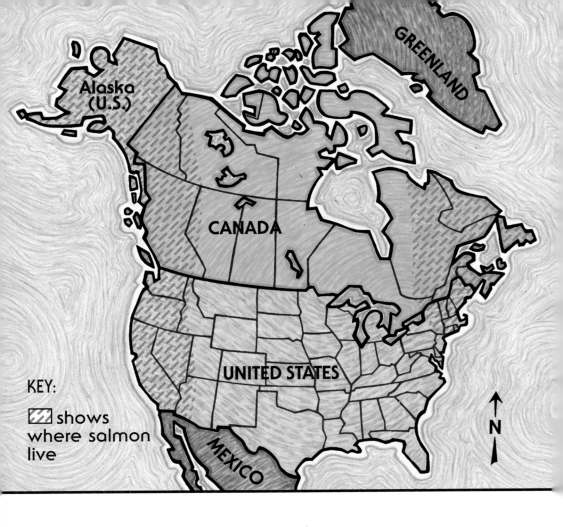

Find your state or province on this map.
Do salmon live near you?

Parts of a Salmon's Body

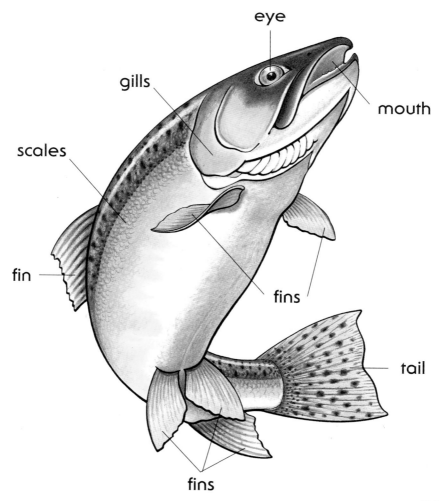

eye

gills

mouth

scales

fin

fins

fins

tail

Glossary

current: the direction in which water flows

fins: parts of a fish's body that help it swim and steer in the water

freshwater: water that is not salty

fry: young salmon

gills: narrow openings on the sides of a fish's head that allow the fish to breathe underwater

predator: an animal that hunts and eats other animals

scales: small pieces of hard skin that cover and protect a salmon

spawn: to produce young

Hunt and Find

- a salmon **digging a nest** on page 11
- salmon **eggs** on pages 12–13
- salmon **hatching** on pages 14–15
- salmon **jumping** on pages 25–26
- a **salmon fry** on page 17
- salmon **swimming** on pages 5, 20, 22–24

About the Author

Mike Dembeck

Kathleen Martin-James was born in Toronto, Ontario. She has lived in many different places across Canada and in the United States. Now she lives in Halifax, Nova Scotia, with her husband, Mike. Kathleen enjoys writing books for children and articles for magazines. She also loves to read, and write stories and poems.

Photo Acknowledgments

Photographs reproduced with permission from: © Natalie Fobes, pp. 3, 4, 5, 6, 11, 14, 15, 17, 19, 20, 23, 31; © Daniel W. Gotshall/Visuals Unlimited, p. 7; © Jeffrey Rich Nature Photographer, pp. 8, 16; © Glenn M. Oliver/Visuals Unlimited, pp. 9, 18; © Gary Schultz, pp. 10, 12, 22, 24, 25, 26; © Ted Clutter/Photo Researchers, Inc., p. 13; © C. P. George/Visuals Unlimited, p. 21; © Linda J. Moore, p. 27. Cover © Natalie Fobes.